LISTENING WITH THE HEART

Dorothy D. France

LISTENING WITH THE HEART

Brings

Healing

and Hope

To Those Who Grieve

DOROTHY D. FRANCE

Dedicated to my beloved late husband,
The Rev. Carl G. France, who lived the words and taught
me to believe that "I can do all things through him who
gives me strength."   (Philippians 4:13)

Acknowledgments

I am indebted to all those who over the years confided in me, sharing their stories of sorrow and pain, and to those who supported me by "listening with their hearts" during my journey of recovery following my own loss.

Special thanks is given to my family, my many friends, colleagues and physicians who shared my journey including Carroll and Bobbie Brown, Tom and Dot Smith, Dolores Gravatt, Beverly and Jerry Wolfe, Carol Snyder, Jackie Grinstead, Marilyn and Chet Workman, Bob and Evelyn Ling, Bob Freed, John Lecky, Russ Johnson, members of the Co-Wed Class of High Street Christian Church in Akron, Ohio and Pastors Ken Kindig, Russ Goldner, Tom Shiflett, Mitch Maxted, Dr. and Mrs. James Grow and Dr. Ted Shaub.

I also wish to thank Sarah Woodford for her contribution of *Gathered at the Table.* Sarah's creative writing talents were highlighted in *Equal Ground,* a literary journal produced in 2003 by her high school creative writing class.

The other quotations, verses, and reflections included in this book were gathered over the years as Carl and I listened to and internalized the wisdom of others during seminars and retreats, or they were shared by friends and colleagues. To the unknown authors, contributors and original sources my thanks, and where appropriate my apologies for not being able to credit the source.

A Listening Heart

Dear Lord, I want a listening heart,
    Not only ears that hear,
    For only when I listen well
    Your presence feels so near.
I want my eyes to see much more,
    Not just a small, small part,
For eyes may not reveal as much
    Seen by a loving heart.
My lips may speak so many words,
    But they may be in vain;
    The listening heart is open to
    Another's grief and pain.
There's so much pain and sorrow, Lord;
    I need to feel you near.
Just give me words and eyes that see
    And, Lord, a heart that hears.
    I thank you for your loving care
    And, Lord, I humbly pray
    For love enough to pass along
    To those along life's way.
Perhaps they need some "comfort" words,
    But that is only part–
    So in the quiet of the hour
    I want a listening heart.

—Gertrude B. McClain

Contents

Introduction

When we focus on others instead of ourselves, it not only benefits others it transforms our lives as well.

The most shattering experience that can befall the human spirit is the death of a loved one. The loss affects your head, heart and spirit. No words, no theory, no formula can numb the immediate and overwhelming pain that has come to your life.

We are never fully prepared for death, whether it comes slowly or suddenly. It seems to signal the end of everything. I know because I have traveled over the long and winding road of recovery.

Most of what you will read in this book comes from my personal experience as I dealt with my own pain and heartache and as I endeavored to help an individual or family deal with loss.

A few years ago my husband and I made the decision to leave our home, family and life-long friends in Virginia and move to Ohio so that we could enjoy a few important years with our daughter and two teenage grandsons; both were active in high school sports and their grandfather, a lifelong sports fan, wanted to be there to cheer them on. They were able to share only one season together before cancer stepped in and shattered our dreams.

Carl and I met during World War II when he was stationed at Camp Pickett, Virginia. He had been preparing for the ministry prior to receiving his invitation to be a part of the military. The minister of my home church somehow learned that he was at the base and invited him to be the guest preacher for a Sunday evening service. It was my turn to play the piano and as fate would have it we sat on the front pew in the sanctuary and picked out hymns that would relate to his message.

It became obvious as the service progressed that he was not only a talented preacher but had a beautiful voice as well. He wasn't bad to look at either! The year following his death I used a hymnbook for my daily devotions. The messages from those hymns and the memories of his singing them as a part of worship gave me strength to face the unknown future.

As time passed I became more and more aware, not only of my own heartache and loneliness, but of the pain and heartache of my daughter, Gail, and my two grandsons, Jason and David. Gail returned immediately to her work as a hospital critical care nurse. The boys returned to their routine of going to school and participating in the demanding training related to their sports activities. It was very obvious that they missed the physical presence of their grandfather in the stands during the games.

During the cold winter months I tried to pick up where "Pa Pa" left off. I became the boys' cheerleader and attended every event I could - football, basketball, wrestling. I also returned to writing. It became my catharsis, enabling me to deal with my anger and fears and helping me to focus on what now had to be faced. As I put some of my feelings on paper it helped ease my anxiety about the future.

Blessed Assurance, a devotional book based on phrases from the hymns we both loved and cherished, was written the year following my husband's death. A year later I joined forces with David and Jason and wrote a little book about football titled, *You Might Be A Football Fan If* . . . In 2003 we shared in the authorship of *You Might Be A Basketball Fan If* . . . The book you now hold in your hands was written with my late husband's assistance. Following his retirement from the pastoral ministry he served as a consultant in the area of death and dying. He organized support groups for the recently bereaved and for parents of children who had committed suicide. He helped organize discussion groups in several local high schools dealing with "teenage suicide."

I didn't realize how extensive his work was until I came across a large file of his notes and observations. In our ministry spanning over fifty years we counseled and shared with many parishioners who had experienced the loss of a spouse, parent, child or friend. Many had lost jobs. One family had their home destroyed by fire. Others lost their self-esteem during a divorce or while dealing with an alcoholic or drug addicted spouse or family member.

Those memories and experiences came back to the forefront of my thinking as I found myself trying to deal with my own grief in a new environment away from my extended family and friends. It seemed that everywhere I had been or would go, individuals would approach me wanting someone to listen to their story and feel their pain. They always wanted to know how I'd managed to keep going and in such an upbeat manner. Sometimes I wanted to tell them that I felt like an earthquake was taking place inside me; that I wasn't nearly as together as it might seem to them. In retrospect, I probably should have told them that I was hurting too.

One day, Jackie, a dear friend, and I were having lunch in a local restaurant. We were reflecting on a discussion we had just had with two members of a craft group in a nearby store. Both had recently lost family members. The woman was grieving over the loss of her husband of 68 years and the young man, the floral designer, had buried his mother only a few days earlier. They wanted someone to assure them that their lives would get better. Both commented that nighttime was the worse and neither was comfortable eating alone, particularly in the evening.

As we ate our lunch, we talked about the conversations we had just had and began to talk about our own pain. Our husbands' passing left us unprepared. Her husband died unexpectedly just after they had played tennis while on vacation. My husband died shortly after being diagnosed with cancer. There was really little time for either of us to prepare ourselves for what was happening and the emptiness that lay ahead. We agreed that no one is ever fully prepared for death whether it comes slowly or suddenly. It can still take months or years to face and feel the pain.

As we prepared to leave the restaurant, Jackie looked across the table at me, paused for a moment, and said, "You have written books on other subjects. I think it's time you wrote a book to help folks like the two of us get on with their lives." I promised her I would give it prayerful consideration.

One day a clergy friend, who visited often to give me support, asked me to tell him more about the special ministry Carl began after his retirement. I explained briefly his ministry with those who were grieving, especially those who had lost a young family member through suicide. He commented that some bereavement counselors suggest that identification with the dead person is a necessary part of the grief process and that identification may be as simple as finishing a project begun with the dead person.

Before his death Carl and I talked often about writing a book on grief. We just never got around to doing it. Now my identification has been made. I hope it will give you the courage to identify and complete your unfinished project as you begin your journey of healing.

What Is So Special About a Table?

Gathered at the table
Smiles and tears resound.
Healing begins.

—*Sarah Woodford*

It is because of my strong feelings about tables and the healing that can take place there that I have chosen to format this book around table settings. Each chapter deals with a particular phase of grief recovery that may take place around a table and presents material useful to both those who are grieving and those who are assisting persons on their grief journey.

Specific information for dealing with the death of a child, how to assist a parent who has lost a child or how to talk to a child about death is not addressed. Many books are currently available that deal with this particular population.

Think for a moment with me about tables. They are everywhere. This piece of furniture more than any other, is the symbol and instrument of fellowship; the bond which binds us together. There are many kinds of tables: dinner tables and picnic tables, card tables and game tables, library tables and office tables, conference tables and peace tables.

We all have a need to belong and be accepted. Gathering around a table gives us that sense of belonging. We gather around tables to eat, study, create, confer, make decisions, enjoy fellowship, laugh and sometimes cry. It doesn't matter whether it is a banquet table or the kitchen table; it can have an extraordinary influence on who we are or who we will become. We are nourished throughout life by friendships often developed around a table.

I realized when I was very young that something special happened at our kitchen table. Our life as a family seemed to intentionally center around that particular table. It was more than a place for eating. Sometimes my mother would do her ironing there. Sometimes we kids would gather around it to do our homework while she was preparing dinner. Sometimes we gathered on cold winter evenings to play games or work a puzzle. No matter what was taking place it always felt like we were a family who cared about each other.

Neighbors and friends sometimes gathered there with us. Whenever anyone in our little town needed a listening ear he or she would come and sit at that table with my dad. Color, age, gender, economic status - none of these mattered. Folks knew they'd always find a "cocked ear" ready to listen and understand.

I learned early on in life that it is somehow easier to share your joys or pain with a friend when you are seated at a table. Perhaps it's because the table is not just a place of physical nourishment but also a place where we can work through our feelings and where our emotional and spiritual needs can be fed through friendships.

I still have that kitchen table made of sturdy oak, its massive legs with deep carved grooves encircling them. Those legs still remind me that they need dusting every Saturday morning. They remind me that time and care must be given so that the table will be ready for gathering around whenever someone needs to be listened to or cared for.

Coming to the table alone can be really hard work following the loss of a loved one. But I am convinced that gathering at a table with family and friends can and will make the pain a little easier. Tables, you see, should be places where we will not only feel welcome but where a sense of active listening and understanding can and will take place.

I have listened to and conferred with many individuals and groups since my husband's death. Listening to their stories of heartache and pain reassured me that I was not alone in my sorrow. Others have the same or similar feelings and longings. Together we acknowledged our feeling of aloneness and the difficulty we had in coping during the evening hours, especially at mealtime.

One woman commented that she used a tray table and always sat in another room so she would not see the empty chair at the kitchen table. "We were used to lingering around the table," she said. "We discussed the events of the day or shared our plans for tomorrow. Sometimes we just sat awhile sipping our coffee or tea, checking the mail or commenting on the news as we read the paper. Often we'd work a puzzle or play a game of cards."

Not all of those who feel loneliness when thinking about the table live in private homes. Many reside in retirement facilities and still find eating alone at a table difficult. One resident helped me to appreciate my own kitchen table.

It was my turn as a church elder to visit Marjorie in the nursing home. I had visited her often but on this particular day I had chosen mid-morning for the visit, thinking that it would not interfere with the early morning schedule, lunch or rest time. After an enjoyable visit I prepared to leave. I knew it was nearing the lunch hour because the residents were beginning to gather around the tables in the dining room. Marjorie insisted that I walk with her to her assigned table. As soon as she was seated she began to beg me to stay and have lunch or at least sit with her while she ate. She said, "It is so lonely and awful to sit at the table and eat by myself. I feel like I can't swallow my food."

An aide brought lunch and sat it before her. Marjorie asked the aide to please bring a lunch for her friend. I declined, but after much negotiating I finally accepted a salad. Marjorie looked at me and smiled as she said, "Now I will try to eat." A little later a nurse walked by and commented on how pleased she was that Marjorie had eaten so much. As she took a bite from her salad Marjorie smiled and replied, "Oh, it just tastes so much better when you are sitting at the table sharing it with a friend."

That's what makes a table so special!

Where Do We Begin
Our Grief Journey?

When a person is born, we celebrate;
When they marry we jubilate;
But when they die we act as if nothing
Has happened.

—*Margaret Mead*

Death has touched us. It is a stranger to no one. How we respond will vary from individual to individual. It will affect us in different ways and the response to our grief and the bereavement that follows will take many shapes and forms. So, where do we begin?

- We begin our grief journey at the beginning by acknowledging that at some time in our lives each of us will embrace death. Some of us may experience the death of a family member or friend early in life. Others may encounter considerable loss over a period of years. Some of us may even live free from the death of a dear one until we reach our senior years.
- We begin by acknowledging that we are all going to die whether we are ready or not. We begin the process of dying the moment we are born. Many of us will remember playing the game of Hide and Seek when we were children. The person chosen to be "it" closed his or her eyes, counted slowly to ten and then called out in a loud voice, "Ready or not here I come." Death is like that. It comes whether we are ready or not.
- We begin by acknowledging that the death of a loved one is always going to be painful and that when the loss occurs we will be faced with unexpected decisions about our own life.
- We begin by acknowledging that dying needs as much attention as all the other things in our life. There is no sense in keeping it hidden until we trip

over it. The choices we make about living, to a great extent if not absolutely, establish the manner in which we will experience dying.

- We begin by acknowledging and trying to understand what grief really is. It does not make any difference how brave and strong we are or think we can be, we must call grief or sorrow by its right name in order to be able to work through it. Each of us may use different words to define it. For me it is best described as "a period during which one can readjust to the environment in which the deceased is missing and start adjusting to life without that person." It is a series of thoughts and feelings which allow us to begin to build a new life.

- We begin by acknowledging that grief is part of being a human being and manifests itself in many more ways than crying, sleeplessness, loss of appetite and general sadness. Other grieving behaviors, so familiar to those of us who have experienced loss, are foreign to those who have not and constitute what one counselor described as "the hidden face of grief." They include things that are said which are sometimes hurtful, questions people ask which seem to be prying for details which we are not ready to discuss, or individuals suggesting to us that "It's time to get on with your life. You've grieved long enough."

- We begin by acknowledging that grief is work. It is exhausting and very emotional. It hurts to be

healed. Grief creates an uneasy and insecure feeling. At first many of us will feel like we are in
limbo. We are neither living in the past or present,
nor looking to the future. We simply feel that we do
not have the strength to get through today much
less think about tomorrow.

- We begin by acknowledging that grieving takes
  time. It is not an illness and there is no magic formula to ease the pain. There seems to be no specific
  beginning or ending point that can be identified as
  normal. There are no road maps or exact blue-
  prints. Dr. Alan D. Wolfelt, Director of the Center
  for Loss and Life Transition in Ft. Collins, Colorado,
  writes that "There is a difference between the head
  and the heart. Hearts need time to catch up with
  what the head knows." We wander alone through
  the empty house, look across the table to an empty
  chair, sleep alone in an empty bed, face the day
  thinking of what might have been or asking why.
  All of these tell us what we already know - that
  things will never be the same again.

- We begin by acknowledging that each of us must
  handle grief in our own way. While there are some
  common stages and responses to grief, each of us in
  the final analysis must grieve on our own time
  table. Our grief cannot be measured by that of another and it cannot be compared to someone else's
  experience.

- Lastly, we must acknowledge that life will go on
  whether we want it to or not, and with or without

us. Our loss does not mean that the relationship ends, it just changes. The pain of our grief may never completely leave but it will taper off and we will be able to move toward wholeness once again.

We *will* find strength for today and bright hope for tomorrow.

Sympathy

Sympathy is your hurt within my heart;
O Friend, may I come in and take your hand.
And say a healing word and have a part
in this your grief? How well I understand!
For I have gone the whole long weary way;
I know how steep the slopes, how rough the road;
But also, Friend, I know there comes a day
When God's own hand will lift your heavy load.
Take heart!–Tomorrow's hills will shine with light,
And happiness again will lave your breast.
Have faith and know that after this dark night
Will come release and peace and needed rest.
Trust now, and God, whose Word is ever true
Is sure to reach a hand to comfort you.

—Source unknown

Tables of Preparation

Bereavement is a strange companion.
It drains us of energy, robs us of our smiles,
renders us incapable of making decisions,
threatens our faith in God and leaves an
emptiness that does let up, but never filled.

—Source unknown

Someone has aptly observed that "Nothing is lonelier than death, unless it is death denied." When we are first confronted with death we find it hard to comprehend what has happened. We have experienced a loss that affects our head, heart and spirit. C. S. Lewis wrote that the death of a beloved is like an amputation. It is traumatic and we cannot think clearly.

The most isolating and frightening part of our grief journey may well be our sense of disorganization and confusion, the searching and yearning, the asking why. We are thrust into making decisions and dealing with unanticipated events for which we are not prepared.

One of the first tables around which we gather will likely be at a funeral home or around our kitchen or dining room table with our pastor or rabbi. Unless our loved one has made pre-death arrangements, immediate decisions must be made regarding the funeral or memorial service. A funeral is the ceremony held in connection with the burial or cremation of the dead. A graveside service may also be held. A memorial service is similar to a funeral service but without the body present and often occurs weeks or months after the death. Decisions must also be made regarding where the service will be held and who will lead and participate in that service.

A few years ago I received a call that my sister-in-law had died suddenly. My husband and I hurriedly packed a few things and made the two-hour trip to be with my brother who was in total shock. The next morning as I sat at the kitchen table with his son and his minister discussing the memorial service, he asked me to give the eulogy. It was not exactly what I wanted to do but something I felt I must do. When the minister's visit was over my nephew came back into the room with tears rolling down his cheeks and said, "I know Dad is in shock but he thinks he's the only one hurting. Doesn't he realize he lost his wife but I lost my mother? He thinks he's alone in his pain." I knew immediately that my eulogy needed to be sensitive to the pain of the entire family.

Our conversation reminded me of a young teenager who punched a hole in the bathroom wall with his fist following the death of his mother. That was the only way he knew to vent his anger. His pain was so deep and rightly or wrongly he felt that most of the attention was being centered on his father's grief.

For many of us the funeral director and staff are the only support system available to us when these immediate and important decisions must be made. Experience has proven that the majority of these facilities have staff trained to listen carefully and offer sympathetic advice and guidance. They are prepared to help us work through and make critical decisions that take into consideration the feelings of all family members.

(Information on the basic services provided by funeral home staff is included in Appendix A.)

Friends and extended family members will be our strongest supporters during this time when funeral arrangements must be made. They can assist by calling the minister or rabbi and making a list of others to be notified of the death. The listing may include not only family members and close friends who live in and out of the immediate area but neighbors, fellow church or club members, employers and/or employees.

It is important that some type of funeral or memorial service be provided. These services are for the living and give us an opportunity to mourn and talk with relatives and friends. Before the viewing of the body we are in a state of disbelief. The service helps us acknowledge the reality of the death, provides us with an accepted venue for our painful feelings and gives testimony of the new life of the deceased. It is perhaps the only time and place during which society will condone our open and outward expression of sadness.

The service also provides a public and traditional means by which we can express our beliefs, thoughts and feelings about death. It offers an opportunity to express and share hope for the living and helps provide for closure as we transition to another stage of life. It encourages us to express our grief in a way that is consistent with our particular cultural and family values. It lends support by allowing us to openly express our faith as well as our beliefs and understandings about life and death itself. As we acknowledge the reality of the death we are enabled to give testimony to the life of the deceased.

Some of us may wish to place a special remembrance, something tangible that the deceased loved, in the casket. Having something special buried with that person is one way of showing affection.

One evening as I stood by the casket in the funeral home giving thanks for the life of the deceased person, her husband came and stood beside me. He quietly whispered, "Have you noticed anything unusual in the casket?" "I don't think so," I replied. He suggested that I stand on tiptoe and take another look. When I did I noticed a small ceramic frog nestled close to her waist. "You're the only one besides family that knows it is there," he said. "I collect frogs. She pretended not to like them but I know this one was her favorite. Whenever she dusted my collection she seemed to hold it a little longer than the others. Would it be all right if I left it there?"

As I placed my arm around him I assured him that not only would it be all right but that he had shown his deep love for her in a beautiful way.

Carol was filled with joy as she shared the good news of the birth of her twin grandchildren with her luncheon group. She expressed concern that the little girl was not doing well and asked for our prayers. During a brief shopping time after lunch she noticed a Beanie Baby "angel bear" on display and purchased it. Several weeks later she received the call that her granddaughter had died. As she prepared to travel to be with family for the service, she commented, "I have decided to place the 'angel' in her casket. It may not be the correct thing to do but she will always be my angel."

Family, friends and co-workers are extremely important as we try to cope with the seemingly impossible things we must face in the days and weeks that lie before us. Their presence at the service provides a time when they can share in our grief and gives them an opportunity to openly and publicly demonstrate their concern and support.

A friend may offer to take charge and invite individuals to assist in answering the door, receiving telephone calls, helping with food by organizing meals and snacks, keeping a listing of those who call, visit, or bring food and offering to care for the children, mow the lawn or run other errands.

Many funeral homes and churches provide a special book for recording information as well as labels for marking food dishes that will need to be returned.

If no one volunteers, we should not hesitate to ask for assistance. Often persons do not volunteer because they may think others were asked and they do not wish to intrude upon our privacy.

Friends can also be helpful in preparing clothing for the deceased as well as items of clothing the family may need for the visitation hours and the funeral service.

Assistance with the children and elderly family members is also appreciated. This may include taking items to the cleaners or perhaps doing the laundry.

When the funeral is over and our support system begins to diminish it is then that we will rely on those special friends and loved ones to stand with us. They will enable us to cope during what may seem like an impossible future.

In addition to the assistance we receive from friends, many funeral homes offer group sessions led by professionals who are trained to assist individuals and families in coping with death. Some also provide special services during holidays or holy days and may provide an ornament engraved with the deceased's name and date, or a similar item for our use on a special occasion.

(Information on support groups is found in Appendix B.)

Tips for friends and supporters.

- Be sensitive and careful about the personal questions you may want to ask regarding the details of the death. Individuals may not feel comfortable when sharing information that seems so very private.
- Be aware of and lend support for other family members, such as children, siblings and grandparents.
- Be careful about what you say. Often it is best to say nothing. Maybe it would be better to just hold their hand, place an arm around them for a moment or simply place your hand on their shoulder. Your body language will often speak louder than the words you speak.

Tables of Hospitality
and Fellowship

You give but little when you give of your possessions.
It is when you give of yourself that you truly give.

—*Kahlil Gibran,* The Prophet

It seems that right after the funeral or memorial service, everyone departs expecting those of us who are mourning to recover on our own as quickly as possible. One of the marked characteristics of that time is our emptiness.

Close friends who do not forget us are extremely important.

It was the day before New Year's Eve. It was very cold and the ground was covered with a blanket of snow. I felt all alone and a bit depressed as I sat at my kitchen table addressing thank you notes to individuals and groups who had made memorial gifts. Intellectually I may have realized that a great many people were living in the midst of doubt and fear but this had little meaning to me at that particular moment in my life.

The telephone rang and I sat there as if frozen and let the answering machine take the call for me. I listened. "Hi. This is Evelyn. I want to talk to you about going with Bob and me to the First Night New Year's Eve event at church. We will pick you up. Give me a call."

The phone rang early on New Year's morning. The machine continued to be my messenger. "Good morning, Dorothy. How are you this morning? I was washing and drying the dishes and thinking about you. Hope you are doing okay. I wanted to let you know that lots of people are thinking about you. We're going to have a good new year, aren't we? Oh, it won't be all a bed of roses but it'll be good. We'll just have to go through the thorns to get to the roses. I'll be thinking about you today and all the tomorrows. We'll get together with friends and go out to eat soon."

I wanted to scream out, "No! I'm sitting here at my kitchen table eating breakfast alone. It isn't going to be a good new year. No! I can't make my own sunshine. My sunshine is gone." But I just could not do it. Both individuals who called knew the pain I was going through because they had been through it themselves.

As I write these words today, I'm grateful to the person who suggested that I keep a notebook close by and write down the calls and messages I received.

One day I shared my phone calls with a neighbor whose wife had died a few weeks earlier. I suggested he might like to jot down his messages for future reading. He said, "Oh yes, I know, but I don't need to write them down. I'll remember. I'll recall the flowers, cards, letters, and the constant ringing of the telephone. But after they stop coming and the flurry of tending to all those necessary and murky details is over, the sudden realization of what has happened will come to the surface and I must be able to deal with them. That's when I'll begin to miss all those people who were here earlier."

I nodded my head in agreement and thought to myself, "Some may be able to remember the specifics of their messages but I'm glad I wrote mine down." Reading and rereading them reminded me that there were people still around who cared. I suggest that you consider making notes too. I assure you they will bring comfort to you later.

It is painful to be alone in your grief but even more so if you are a teenager. One of my grandsons surprised me with a visit one afternoon. As he took a soft drink from the refrigerator his voice quivered as he told me that one of his friend's father had died suddenly the evening before. We sat down at the table and he told me about Mike, who lived with his father. He said he and several friends had decided to take turns spending the night so that Mike would not be alone.

As he stood to leave, he removed his billfold from his pocket and took out a piece of paper that had been folded into a square. He unfolded it and handed it to me. It was the bulletin from his grandfather's memorial service. "I've been carrying this ever since the funeral," he said. "When I'm down I take it out and read it. It helps me especially when I'm feeling alone." We hugged each other and cried; cried and hugged some more. He needed me and I needed him too. He understood the pain his friend was feeling because he had felt the pain when his grandfather died.

While it is painful to be alone in our grief it is also hard for others who seek to give us comfort. Relatives and friends who intended to remain in close contact may have found themselves uncomfortable and at a loss for what to say. Individuals who have not dealt with their own concerns about death find it hard to help someone else. Even those who have been through a similar experience understand that each situation is different and fear being inadequate.

Words seem to be fragile vessels when one tries to communicate and help others with the reality of grief. Maybe being there to support us is more than they are capable of handling at the time. Even though we are grieving we need to be patient. Perhaps as time passes our friends will come to realize that each of us at one time or another has been the recipient of kindness from someone else. The memories of that hospitality will give them the strength to help us at our time of need.

Individuals have often said to me, "I do not know what to do or say, so I do nothing." My response usually is to assure them that talking is not the first priority; their presence and understanding is what counts. As we share dessert around a table in an ice cream shop with a group of friends after church or a concert, we can listen and give support without ever speaking. We can always smile as we grasp their hand or place a hand on their shoulder for a brief moment.

When we lose a loved one, we are left with an empty space. There is an irreducible loneliness in our life. The focus upon our period of bereavement is a necessary re-organization process which will bring with it change, and perhaps instability and pain. Redefining one's role in a culture that is uncomfortable with death is difficult but we must eventually take steps to develop a new lifestyle.

Sometimes we find it hard to make what others may consider simple decisions. Our family and friends find us saying yes or agreeing to do something one minute when we honestly meant to say no. When we change our mind and refuse to go out after arrangements have been made for a special evening, they lose patience with us.

Over the years as I have visited with grieving individuals the comment heard most often, other than that they hated eating at the table alone and that the nights were the worst, is that they wished that people would not say to them, "don't be depressed" or " things will get better," or "don't you think it is time to get on with your life."

We who grieve are aware of the expectations that others have that we quickly recover and present ourselves as restored individuals. The management of these expectations, however, does not mean that our mourning process itself has ended.

When our status changes from couple to single through death, we are left to function alone and find it hard to accept an invitation, especially to dinner. We become aware that many of those dining in the restaurants are couples. Each time we sit at a table we are reminded of the painful reality that the one we loved is gone and will never return. At the same time, we may be reminded that time will enable us to heal and learn to cope once again.

Many of us who mourn find ourselves drawn to public places like malls or shopping centers, bookstores or perhaps libraries. We do so in hopes that we will hear the sound of a voice or the sight of a person that seems similar to our loved one. Somehow it makes us feel the person is still close by. It gives us a sense of presence.

Being in a public place may also cause us to experience what one counselor refers to as "trigger events." We may see a couple coming toward us holding hands, laughing and talking. It brings back memories. Maybe we have heard friends who are widows or widowers comment that after years they still have not adjusted to having to function in society as a single person. Their words have extra meaning for us now and may bring pain that cannot easily be put aside.

Sooner or later we will come to realize that no matter how much socializing we do, most of us will face alone the harsh reality of death. We will instinctively try to mask the inner pain. One of the best ways to work through our hurt as we move toward the reality of our loss will be to talk out our thoughts and fears. We will surely need support. If family and friends do not reach out to us then we need to reach out to them, realizing that the need to talk through our feelings is a normal part of the grief process.

We all need to be given time to keep the memory of our loved one in the forefront of our thinking. If we know that someone will be visiting, perhaps we should encourage the individual to bring pictures of a special occasion so those memories can be shared. Placing them on the table before us as we sip our coffee or tea will enable us not only to share precious moments from the past but may also encourage us to start a new chapter of memories.

A friend called on a day that hadn't been very pleasant for either one of us. We tried to bring cheer to each other. As we closed our conversation she added, "You know there is nothing that can take the place of the human connection."

Those words linger with me yet. They were right on target! A friend's physical presence as we gather about a table will convey far more than any words that we speak.

Tips for those who grieve.

- Be patient with yourself.
- Call a friend when you feel the need to talk to someone.
- Be mindful of other family members who are also grieving.

- Ask for help with tasks that seem too difficult to handle alone.
- Do not feel embarrassed if you have to cancel an engagement.

Tips for friends and supporters.

- Assistance will be needed the most during the weeks and months that follow the funeral or memorial service.
- Special attention should be given to children and teenagers who have lost a parent.
- If you promise to visit, to call, to assist with a particular task, make sure you do not forget. Most bereaved individuals will not call to ask for assistance.
- Care can be given in many ways: through a personal visit, a telephone call, a note, a flower.
- Be available to provide transportation to the grocery store or to a doctor's appointment.
- Provide assistance with addressing thank you notes, or returning dishes to those who brought food.
- Stop by with a few cookies and stay for coffee or tea, or pick up a pizza and salad and stay for dinner.
- Learn to listen and give support without ever speaking as you enjoy dessert with a group of friends. Give the person a warm smile as you grasp their hand for a brief moment.

Tables of Understanding and Encouragement

We go this way but once,
So why not make the journey worth-while.
Giving to those who travel with us
A helping hand, a cheer, a smile?

—*Source unknown*

Society seems to encourage the discussion of almost any aspect of human experience with relative openness and candor from growing up to growing old but when it comes to grief such open conversation seems to cease.

This continuing gap between the cultural distortions concerning grief and the private realities shared by those of us who grieve, has allowed the true face of grief to remain hidden from view. In doing so, it has also deflected caring persons away from the genuine needs of those who are moving through the grief process.

It seems ironic that just at the time we need support the most, those around us think we should be "all better." Everyone seems to want us to hurry up; to rush through like we are going through the express lane in the grocery store.

Friends tell us that "It is time to get on with life." To us it may feel like all they think we need to do is to put a bright colored band-aid over our hurt like we put on a child's knee or elbow to make the "boo-boo" go away and bring instant healing.

What many do not realize is that in order for us to even begin to rebuild our lives we need their support. We need each other; we need to talk, to share tears, and be touched. We need a place where we can express our feelings without fear of isolation or judgment. At times we feel that we are walking alone and in the dark and need a safe environment where we can be with family and friends. We need the time and a place to release our feelings.

When friends or family members, who have not faced death themselves, try to conceive of what other individuals feel, many still believe that grieving people cry all the time, cannot sleep at night, have no appetite and appear to be sad. The simple fact is that sooner or later we must sleep and eat and eventually we will learn to control our tears and looks of sadness when with others.

Dr. Alan D. Wolfelt, Director of the Center for Loss and Life Transition, suggests that "No one experiencing the pain of grief can move toward healing or reconciliation without being understood by at least one person."

He suggests that helping begins with an individual's ability and willingness to be an active listener; *to listen with the heart.* Listening is indeed a critical part of empathy and understanding.

Those who listen need to understand that sometimes we feel like we are in a swamp and can't find our way out. Our day may start out fairly upbeat and then something happens. We're not sure what, but something triggers a change and what began as a good day turns into a bad one.

Our feelings come in waves like being at the ocean. It is like we're standing on the beach with our feet barely in the water. We turn to look at a seashell or a seagull as it hops away and all of a sudden a wave rolls over our feet, almost knocking us to the ground.

Throughout our grief journey the more we are able to tell our story of the death itself and share memories of the person who has died, the more likely we will be able to reconcile our grief. It is important, not only for us but for those who would listen, to remember that we all do not move through grief at the same pace. We have to set our own timetable. Friends and family are needed who will help us do the work of mourning and be supportive wherever we may be in our journey at any given moment.

A person's physical presence about a table and the desire to listen to us without being judgmental enables us to deal with our loss. We need caring friends who will provide support through their gift of interest, time and energy. The care may be temporary but, oh, so very critical to our healing.

We who grieve must also be open to receive help; we must be willing to allow others to listen to us as we cry and pour out our sorrow over and over again. When listening takes place, we as individuals or as a family may indicate not only through our words but also our body language ways in which others can help us during this extraordinarily difficult time.

Sometimes when we are distraught we tend to push away our friends. Perhaps it is because we truly want to be alone; perhaps not for long but at least for that moment. We turn down invitations to dinner, a play or maybe a movie. Sometimes only a few friends continue to come through for us even if we haven't pushed them away. When this happens we need to remember that it is perfectly acceptable to ask for help; sometimes individuals are hesitant because they do not wish to appear overbearing. Sometimes it is because they, too, sense that we need to be alone!

Some people may try to distance us from the possessions that belonged to the one who has died. This behavior fits with the tendency in our culture to move away from grief instead of moving toward it. Embracing the comfort provided by familiar objects may actually help move us toward reconciliation and healing. Simply giving away the possessions does not equate with healing nor does keeping them mean we have to "create a shrine." One of my dearest friends found great comfort in wearing one of her husband's favorite sweaters whenever she went for a walk. Some thought this strange but as time passed she eventually hung it in her closet. When the time was right she passed it on to a clothing bank.

My late husband enjoyed playing golf not only with friends but also with his grandsons. When we shared vacations he always invited the two of them to join him for his morning game. He not only enjoyed their company but worked in a little instruction as well. After his death several friends inquired about purchasing his equipment. I kept telling them, "I'll let you know when I'm ready." I have never regretted those words.

One day David came by with one of his friends. "Could I please borrow Pa Pa's golf clubs? We're going to hit a few balls." I was so excited I could hardly speak as I led him to the basement. I watched the expression on his face as he gently picked up the bag. I suggested that he clean them up a bit; they had been sitting for several years. He cleaned and polished the irons and clubs and carefully placed each one back into the divider from which it had been taken. He was excited to find some balls and tees along with a towel still hanging on the bag. When he had finished he gave me a hug, placed the bag over his shoulder and walked with his friend through the garage to his car. "I'll see you later," he said. He left not only carrying a golf bag but also the wonderful memories of his golfing days with his grandfather. How thankful I was that I had listened to my own heart.

Our own internal clock will tell us when it is time to begin rearranging closets and disposing of clothing that belonged to the deceased. Some find it helpful to dispose of items one bag or box at a time. A friend suggested I place a shopping bag or box in my closet. Each day I should try to put an item or two in the bag. When it was full I should replace it with an empty one and immediately put the overflowing one in the trunk of my car. When I was ready it could then be taken to an appropriate agency where the items would provide comfort to someone else.

Friends who realize that they cannot take away our pain, but who let their genuine concern and caring show, help us the most as we move toward healing. Two fellow clergy came almost daily following my husband's death. Even though we often sat around the table in silence as we nibbled on donuts or cookies they had brought, their presence continued to demonstrate what they had promised on their first visit when they said, "We'll help you get through this one step at the time."

One step at a time. That's the key. Move at your own pace by taking one step at a time!

Tips for those who grieve.

- There is no right or wrong way to grieve.
- Go slowly and be patient with yourself. We do not all move through grief at the same pace.
- Take the time you need to be alone.

- Be gentle with yourself as you talk about your grief.
- Be tolerant of your inability to function at optimum levels. Be with people you find supportive and comforting.
- Eliminate unnecessary stress. Do not let others keep you busy with things beyond what you are ready and willing to do. Keeping busy can often increase stress and postpone your expression of grief.
- Embrace the comfort of familiar objects.
- Be open to receiving help.
- You will know when it is the right time to dispose of possessions.
- Discourage yourself from making any critical changes or hasty decisions like selling the house or moving to another community.

Tips for friends and supporters.

- Be sensitive to the grievers' timing as they try to fully acknowledge the reality of death. Help can be provided without saying anything.
- Give them the time and space they need to be alone.
- Share a favorite memory of the person or relate the qualities that you valued in the deceased individual.
- Listen non-judgmentally and with permissiveness and acceptance.
- Encourage the griever to realistically review and talk about the deceased and their mutual relationship. At the same time be aware that some feelings may be too personal to share.

- Be aware of all the family members who are grieving. When someone loses a spouse, there may be children who have lost a mother or father, or a sibling who has lost a brother or sister.
- Write a personal note if a visit cannot be made. At the appropriate time encourage the griever to find rewarding new things to do and people to invest in; help make their life livable again.
- Do not forget to plant the seed of hope that someday the pain will decrease.
- As you gather about the table with your family or friends, make sure it is a table of support and encouragement rather than of judgment.

Tables of Celebration— Holidays and Holy Days

And you would accept the seasons of your heart,
    even as you have always
    accepted the seasons
    that pass over your fields.
And you would watch with serenity
    through the winters of your grief.

—Kahlil Gibran, The Prophet

Holiday seasons, after losing someone you love, often represent the most difficult time for the ones who remain. It is natural for those of us who grieve to dread seasons which are intended to be times of joy, family togetherness and gift giving. We are not prepared for the depth of the experience.

Most holidays are family or national events and generally have the momentum of history or tradition to carry them. Holidays often have an agenda, an accepted set of activities to celebrate the event: fireworks, a birthday cake, a Christmas tree, a menorah or the decorating of Easter eggs with grandchildren. These special occasions cause us to focus on the sense of loss that is totally unlike that felt during the daily routine of just living.

Friends and neighbors will observe these special days even if we try not to. There are reminders of Christmas or other holidays everywhere as the world prepares for a particular season. Advertisements fill the newspapers and magazines and call out to us over the radio and television. In the stores and restaurants there are decorations and displays. There is a difference in the way our friends and casual acquaintances greet us. We can sense the anticipation in their voices.

The full sense of the loss of someone we loved never occurs all at once. The onset of a holiday forces us to acknowledge that the person who was a vital part of our life is no longer present and that much our life has been changed forever.

The anticipation of the holidays will naturally bring with it questions and concerns. Some family members may find it difficult to grieve together especially around a holiday table that brings back memories and opens up wounds that are still fresh with sadness. It is even more difficult if individual members are at different stages in the grief process.

Getting ready will be painful as we realize that we will set one less plate at the table or hang one less stocking to be emptied in wonder at Christmas. There will be one less birthday to celebrate and no more anniversaries to share with our partner. Even sporting events will be different. Those that were shared as family will not seem as jubilant at victory time.

While other hearts are filled with laughter, we now find it painful to even smile. The gift we most desire cannot be ours, not this Christmas or Thanksgiving or birthday or anniversary or any celebration yet to come.

Someone observed that your heart may be hungrier than your body on a holiday or at those times when you are sharing a special occasion with family or close friends.

For me, my heart's hunger was more intense at sporting events. My heart and my head were forced to come together and confront the sad reality of what had happened. My husband would never be there again to share the exciting moments as his grandsons participated.

At times I had to really search my heart and monitor my mood in order to find a reason to be grateful. To others the reason was obvious, but when your heart is heavy the weight of your grief clouds out all reason and clarity. It is then that we have to learn to plan ahead, recognize that we need support and try to surround ourselves with those who will understand and love us in spite of our ingratitude. If dining out and reliving the game with friends was a part of celebrating in the past, rather than declining an invitation, perhaps it would be wise to suggest a different restaurant or snack bar where you can begin to form new memories.

Our holiday observances become intimate as we personalize them with our own traditions. These are the moments that enrich life; these are the special memories that intensify our loss. We have every right to have feelings of emptiness and sadness. We will still miss the presence of our loved one even when sharing in meals that are served buffet style with informal seating. Unfortunately, many of those who are around us at the table may try to take these feelings away. Some may feel that their job is to distract us from our memories rather than helping us to be as comfortable as possible at this particular time in our life.

The resurgence of normal, temporary denial of our loss may also occur when we visit vacation locations where we had joined with family and friends for fun times together. I found it helpful to return the first time to our favorite holiday location with a close friend who shared the same love of that particular vacation spot. There I knew I could talk freely, reminiscence and even shed tears when I needed to, knowing she would understand.

When my oldest grandson graduated from high school, each senior was asked to bring a picture which would be flashed on a screen as each one walked across the stage to receive the diploma. His mother kept asking him if he had selected a picture and he assured her that he had. She just didn't know what it was, nor would he tell her. We were surprised, but very pleased and proud, when he walked across the stage while the large picture of him as a young boy sitting under the Christmas tree with his grandfather appeared on the screen. The crowd showed their pleasure as well. The memories were there and he wasn't embarrassed to admit it. It was his way of having his Pa Pa there with him.

As the events in our life continue to change, either for the good or the bad, we must learn to look into the future. It is there that God has a great gift for us. We will not know what it is, because it will be wrapped with time yet to come. Any depression that comes with our "holiday grief" can ultimately be used to move ahead, to assess old ways of being and to make plans for the future.

The only time there is, is now. Like it or not, our life is our song, and we must learn to choose the tune and write the words ourselves.

Tips for those who grieve.

- Don't let anyone try to take away your grief during the holiday season. Decide how much of the holiday you can handle. Allow yourself time to think about and acknowledge your loss and realize your holiday may have both happy and sad moments.
- Listen to your heart and only do the things that feel right for you.
- Be kind to yourself. Try not to worry about what others think.
- The preparation time may actually turn out to be worse than the day itself. If addressing greeting

cards and signing only your name, for example, is too much, perhaps it should be postponed until another year.

- If the thought or act of shopping is upsetting, consider giving cash or ordering gifts by mail or the Internet.
- Compromise until you can come to a comfortable conclusion about any holiday. One day you will be able to function well again, so do not force yourself to do what you really don't want to do. After all, it is not written in stone that you must do things a certain way.
- Keep the memories. Those that were made in love can never be taken away from you and are perhaps the best legacies that exist after a death. Instead of ignoring them, share them with understanding family and friends.
- Light a candle to remember your loved one. As the candle shines, invite those present to share a memory of a previous holiday.

Tips for friends and supporters.

- Be sensitive to the fact that the days and perhaps weeks prior to the holiday may be more difficult than the day itself.
- Offer to help with any decorating the person may wish to do while being sensitive to the individual's wishes if the offer is declined.
- Send an appropriate floral arrangement.

- Offer to assist with addressing cards or making phone calls to friends and relatives.
- Volunteer to be a "personal shopper" or accompany the individual on a shopping trip or to the post office.
- Drop by with cookies or other holiday treats. Bring something special if there are young children in the home.
- Do not insist that the individual or family attend social events unless they feel ready to attend.

Tables of Adjustment and Renewal

You cannot prevent birds of sorrow flying over
  your head.
But you can prevent them from building nests in
  your hair.

—Chinese Proverb

Some days when things seem to be moving at a snail's pace and I seem to be going nowhere in my journey toward recovery, I'll turn to my folder of treasured cards and notes and find tucked away some words of wisdom waiting to be re-discovered.

On a piece of yellowing paper I found these words:

"The Chinese characters that depict the word 'crisis' are two symbols, side by side, one for danger and one for opportunity. There is something positive that can be gained from every negative event or crisis. The choices we make about our own recovery will determine whether or not the loss we experience is a totally negative one."

Most of us take happiness and sunny days for granted. Sadness and rainy days are unwelcome. When life goes along with a song, we take it as normal, but when life tumbles in and troubles come we think something strange is happening to us. We think of joy, success and comfort as our due. Sorrow, failure and hardship we think of as injustices thrust upon us.

But life has rhythm; every mountain has its valleys and every wave crest is followed by a trough. Life will always be an unending journey of ups and downs, of mountains to climb and valleys to enjoy, of challenges to be met and successes to be celebrated. Our attitude toward suffering will be different when we see this suffering as a normal part of living and not as an imposition.

Surely by now we realize that we are not alone in our grief. Millions grieve over losses of a thousand kinds. None of us will ever completely "get over" our loss, but we can work to reconcile ourselves to living with it. Acknowledging and moving toward and through our sadness is healthier than attempting to repress or deny it.

Grieving is a necessary step in our journey of letting go. At some point we will come to realize that some hard, thorny days are normal. Sometimes God does not remove the thorn, but instead gives us the patience to endure the pain. Our own personal relationship with a higher being, whatever form that may take, will provide steadfastness and the inner strength needed to move forward on difficult days. It will provide the stamina necessary for keeping pace with the demands that come to us and give us the determination required to meet and overcome the obstacles that stand in our way.

Each of us will learn in time to own or claim our own needs and we will learn how to be gracious in our sorrow. Eventually we see the miracle of our own life, shattered as it is, and recall the joyful moments of love which filled our life. Some of the things we had hoped to do will not get done and all of our dreams will not be fulfilled.

Somehow we will learn to take the activities of each day one at a time. Somehow as time passes we will be able to sit at the table alone and appreciate the memories. To some this may seem like just plodding along but for others it will be another step toward adjustment and renewal. As time passes, our energy will be revived and we will once again not only love ourselves but others as well. Our roles will change and our titles may change too. As our bitterness and pain eases we will grow in compassion and under-standing. We will sense the hurt and feel the need to care for someone other than ourselves. We will experience the joy of being needed. We will be enabled to move from de-spair to hope.

Someone once observed that grief can take care of itself, but to get the full value of a joy you must have someone to divide it with. This is so true. A friend told me one day that when I was able to share my favorite dessert with someone else I would be on my way toward recovery. She was right! The only thing we are in charge of is our own heart.

As you come to the end of this book, and as your sorrow becomes a little easier to bear, it is my prayer as the author that you can now say with me:

I can move on now
    As if carried on the wings of God's angels.
I can turn my sorrows into joy
    And share my faith and trust with those around me.
I can once again see the twinkle in the stars above me.
I can now embrace the hope of a brighter day as
    reflected from the moon's light.
I can feel the warmth of the sun as its rays beam
    down upon me.

I can be refreshed by the falling rain,
   inspired by the beauty of the budding flowers,
   the changing colors of the leaves,
   and the beauty of the snow as it cleanses the earth.
I can and will remember that life never is going to be
   perfect; it was not before and will not be now.

—Adapted, source unknown

Teach Us To Listen

Teach us to listen
to sounds larger than our own heartbeat,
that endure longer
than our own weeping in the dark.

Give us quiet moments:
so we may hear the grief of the wordless
    stranger,
the breathing of those who are walled away
from the rest of us.

Draw us close to the unseen child
so as we may feel its bony hunger.

Let the new idea speak
unafraid, its meaning to us
and let us speak to it, also without fear.
And give us the humility and power
to hear quickly
the little green seed of hope sprouting
lest we trample it not knowing it is here.

> —*Lillian Smith, CWU Board of*
> *Managers Program, Nazareth,*
> *Kentucky, April 4-6, 1974*

APPENDIX A

Services of the Funeral Director

The funeral director will listen and listen carefully to your individual pain. Sympathetic advice, emotional support and the specific information needed as you complete the relationship with the one who has died will be provided.

When death occurs, regardless of the hour, contact your funeral director and minister/rabbi immediately. The director's main function is to assist with the necessary details of the funeral process. Your minister or rabbi will want to be with you during this difficult time. If the death occurs in a hospital or other health facility, the staff will arrange to have the body removed to the funeral home. If the deceased is to be sent to a distant location for burial, the staff will make all necessary arrangements for transportation, service and burial at that destination.

Services provided by the funeral director may include the following:

- Assist with funeral arrangements including visiting hours, funeral or memorial service and interment.
- Provide for care and custody of the body.
- Assist with the selection of a casket and a vault if desired.
- Coordinate details with the clergy or other spiritual leader.
- Notify any fraternal orders or other organizations and coordinate their participation in service.
- Provide for the music requested, if appropriate.
- Assist in preparing and placing the obituary and funeral notices in the newspaper(s) of your choosing. (It is advisable to supply the director with written information.)
- Contact friends of the deceased to serve as casket bearers.

- Assist in making arrangements for cemetery space, grave opening and closing and any special flowers desired.
- Arrange transportation for the family prior to, during and after the funeral.
- Supervise and direct the funeral or memorial service.
- Accompany family on follow-up visits to the grave as requested. Secure necessary permits and death certificates as required for services and for the filing of insurance claims and Social Security death benefits.
- Assist in filing a claim for survivor benefits under the Social Security Act.
- Help in completing insurance claim forms.
- Follow up after the funeral and provide practical assistance with unforeseen concerns.
- Assist and provide support in making adjustments through a support group or other appropriate means.

APPENDIX B

Support Groups

We need not walk alone . . .
We reach out to each other with love and
understanding and with hope . . .
We come together from all walks of life,
from many different circumstances . . .
We need not walk alone.

—*Credo, The Compassionate Friends*

It is painful to be alone in our grief but it is also difficult for those who seek to give us comfort. Individuals do not know what to say or do unless they have been through a similar situation, and even then it is still difficult.

The task of grieving is often eased with the help of others through small groups in which individuals support one another. Those attending may be strangers meeting for the first time. (Church groups may be the exception but even then members may recognize faces but not know each other on a personal level.) It does not take long, however, for those in the group to become friends. The traditional life-long friend might be more likely to tell us to "be strong" or "move on with life" while one of the individuals in a group will just pass the box of tissues without offering us advice.

One of the most important benefits provided by a support group is the permission to grieve. The Group allows us to listen while others share, and permits us to express our own innermost feelings if we wish. As individuals we may not talk or interact at first but soon we will feel free to enter into the discussion.

The individuals in our group will also provide support as we encourage and assist each other in learning how to accept and deal with our loss. Talking about what has happened, being with others who have been through a similar experience, and having our feelings accepted and heard are things that we all need. The sharing also encourages us to talk about the past and present and helps us to begin to focus on our future as well.

Support groups are offered in most communities by local funeral homes, hospitals, health facilities and churches. Local and regional newspapers often provide a listing of both formal and informal groups such as New Wings or New Beginnings groups that share meals together on a regular basis.

Touching Shoulders

There's a comforting thought at the close of the day,
When I'm weary and lonely and sad,
That sort of grips hold of my poor old heart
And bids it be merry and glad.
It gets in my being and it drives out the blues,
And finally thrills through and through.
It is just a sweet memory that chants the refrain:
"I'm glad I touched shoulders with you!"

Did you know you were brave, did you know you were
    strong?
Did you know there was one leaning hard?
Did you know that I waited and listened and prayed,
And was cheered by your simplest word?

Did you know that I longed for that smile on your face,
For the sound of your voice ringing true?
Did you know I grew stronger and better because
I had merely touched shoulders with you?

I am glad that I live, that I battle and strive
For the place that I know I must fill;
I am thankful for sorrows; I'll meet with a grin
What fortune may send, good or ill.
I may not have wealth, I may not be great,
But I know I shall always be true,
For I have in my life that courage you gave
When once I rubbed shoulders with you.

—Author unknown

Meditations

Be still, Relax!
Let go and let God restore your soul.
Sit in quietness and relate to him your every need.
It is his will to give you peace and comfort.

Remember: "They who wait upon the Lord shall renew their strength; they shall run and not be weary, they shall walk and not faint." (Isaiah 40:31)

One of the hardest things for many of us to do is to sit and be still. Our bodies and minds are so programmed to going and doing, to staying busy. We can't get our body and mind to slow down, much less relax. Following heart bypass surgery my cardiologist insisted that one of the things I had to do when I went home was to have bed rest for at least an hour each afternoon. I didn't have to sleep. I just had to "lay still" for an hour. Then he said, "I know this will be hard for you to do. I guess we'll have to Velcro you to the bed to keep you there."

Being still is hard for many following the death of a loved one or close friend. There are so many decisions and choices to be made; so many tasks to complete; so many people to greet; so many tears that won't stop flowing; so many questions to be asked for which there are no immediate answers. There are so many times of feeling all alone that we just cannot cope with sitting in silence and listening to our own heart beat.

But in time, you will be ready. When you are, set aside a time each day to feel the beat of your own heart. The beat continues but it slows down when we take the time to be quiet.

Meditation is not having great thoughts, but receiving and loving the words you hear and letting them shape your life. Select one of the following as your focus for a day or a week. You may find it helpful to record your thoughts and feelings.

Day 1

"Rejoice in your hope, be patient in tribulation, be
constant in prayer."   (Romans 12:12)

Today as I pray, I will place my life in God's hands.

*O Lord, I'm too upset to face the harsh realities; too tired
to think about anything except getting through today.
Help me to turn my heartache over to you. I know that if I
fold my hands in prayer you will open yours to receive
them. Help me to place my future in your hands that I may
feel the strength that will come from your touch. Keep me
and guide me through this difficult day. Amen.*

List the tasks that you must face today. Ask God to
guide you as they are completed.

Tasks I need to complete today.

1. _____

2. _____

3. _____

4. _____

5. _____

6. _____

7. _____

8. _____

9. _____

10. _____

Day 2

"Even these may forget, yet, I will not forget you. Behold, I have graven you on the palms of my hands." (Isaiah 49:15, 16)

Today I will sit in silence that I may "listen" and receive strength.

O Lord, why is it so hard for me to be alone? Is it because in solitude I am reminded of the struggles that no one else knows about except you? When I am forced to sit alone and wait, is it to help me find the patience that can turn to trust? Today I am anxious about many things. I know that my anxiety will not take away my sorrow. Please assure me that you will not forget me; that in quietness and trust I shall receive strength for all the tomorrows I must face. Amen.

List the struggles and pain that now lie heavy on your heart. Beside each write the name of an individual with whom you may share that burden.

Things with which I am struggling.

1. _____

2. _____

3. _____

4. _____

5. _____

6. _____

7. _____

8. _____

9. _____

10. _____

Day 3

"God is our refuge and strength, a very present help in trouble. Therefore we will not fear though the earth should change."   (Psalm 46:1, 2)

Today I will sit quietly and yield to your touch.

Today, O Lord, I will surrender to you all the things I cannot change. I will surrender my weaknesses that you may remold them into strengths. I will yield to your healing power, your forgiveness and your restoring love. Amen.

List the things you cannot change and surrender them over to God.

The things I cannot change.

1. _____

2. _____

3. _____

4. _____

5. _____

6. _____

7. _____

8. _____

9. _____

10. _____

Day 4

"Have no anxiety about anything, but in everything by prayer and supplication with thanksgiving let your request be known to God . . . Lo, I am with you always."   (Philippians 4:6; Matthew 28:20)

Today I will remember that I do not walk alone. I will feel your presence through the love and touch of my family and friends.

O Lord, today I will remember that I may feel lonely but I am not alone. Open my eyes and ears and awaken my heart that I may be aware of those who care about me. Help me to put my sorrow into words knowing that others will understand. Amen.

List the names of family and friends who will walk with you.

Family members and friends on whom I can rely.

1. _____

2. _____

3. _____

4. _____

5. _____

6. _____

7. _____

8. _____

9. _____

10. _____

Day 5

"He has sent me to bind up the brokenhearted."
(Isaiah 61:1)

Today I will turn my heartaches over to you.

O Lord, I know that neither broken bones nor a broken heart heals quickly. As I turn my hurts over to you help me to be aware that you will not be surprised by the needs I am expressing. You know me even better than I can ever know myself. When I am angry and resentful, enable me to forgive as you have forgiven me. Amen.

List the things that invoke anger and cause hurt to return. Note how you will deal with them.

Things that cause me to become angry.

1. _____

2. _____

3. _____

4. _____

5. _____

6. _____

7. _____

8. _____

9. _____

10. _____

Day 6

"Therefore do not be anxious about tomorrow . . .
Let the day's own trouble be sufficient for the day."
(Matthew 6:34)

Today I will reflect on the times when my faith was
tested.

*O Lord, you know that sometimes I can be a worrier.
Sometimes I cause anxiety within myself because I become anxious about things over which I have no control.
I know that what I ask for in prayer today may not be
granted this day. But I also know that you will answer my
plea in your own time and way. Help me to grow stronger
one day at a time. Guide me that I may keep on believing
and not give up. Amen.*

Reflect and note what has brought you through difficult times in the past. Remember them as
strengths.

Things that have helped me in the past.

1. _____

2. _____

3. _____

4. _____

5. _____

6. _____

7. _____

8. _____

9. _____

10. _____

Day 7

"I will never fail you nor forsake you."
(Hebrews 13:5)

Today I will turn over to you my fears and disappointments.

O Lord, you know that I have many private fears. I am afraid to share them with others lest they perceive me as being weak. Some days I want to be left alone and on other days I fear having to someday live alone. On other days I feel alone even when I am in a crowd. Sometimes I fear that when my initial grief and hurt has eased my family and friends will be too busy living their own lives to spend time with me. Let painful memories of the past fade away that I may face tomorrow unafraid. Amen.

Think about your private fears. List them and address them one by one in the days to come.

My private fears.

1. _____

2. _____

3. _____

4. _____

5. _____

6. _____

7. _____

8. _____

9. _____

10. _____

Day 8

"Well done, good and faithful servant; you have
been faithful over a little, I will set you over much."
(Matthew 25:21)

Today I will be thankful for the little things.

*O Lord, I know that it isn't the big things that matter. It's
the little acts of kindness. A smile on a difficult day, the pat
on the back for a small task accomplished, the unexpected
gift from a secret pal, a telephone call on a rainy day, the
slice of my favorite pie shared by a neighbor or the visit received when I was really lonely. I pray that in time I will be
grateful for all the little things that are giving me strength
and will one day be able to share in a similar way with others who are in need. Help me to be grateful, Lord, even for
the little things. Amen.*

Give thanks for the little things and list them as a
reminder for the days yet to come.

Little things for which I am thankful.

1. _____

2. _____

3. _____

4. _____

5. _____

6. _____

7. _____

8. _____

9. _____

10. _____

Day 9

"Having gifts that differ according to the grace given to us, let us use them."   (Romans 12:6)

Today I will be grateful for the talents and gifts you give to others and to me.

O Lord, I have been told that you give gifts of both the head and the heart. I have seen evidence of these as family and friends have been caring both for my physical and spiritual needs. Right now my mind is filled with only bitterness and negative thoughts. I look around me and I wonder if there will be any strength left to do for myself much less to share with others. Deep down I know in my heart that if I would but empty my life of negative thoughts you would fill me again with the promise of better things to come. Instill within me the ability to give thanks for all my gifts. As I listen to the joys and hurts of my own heart may I hear and respond to the hurts of others. Amen.

Whisper a prayer of thanksgiving as you list your talents and gifts.

My talents and gifts.

1. _____

2. _____

3. _____

4. _____

5. _____

6. _____

7. _____

8. _____

9. _____

10. _____

Day 10

"I will give thanks to the Lord with my whole heart;
I will tell of all thy wonderful deeds."   (Psalm 9:1)

Today I will remember the good and positive things
in my life.

*O Lord, right now there is so much pain in my life. Please
quiet my trembling heart long enough for me to recognize
and be grateful for the joys of the past; for my family and
friends, for the laughter and excitement of children, for the
fellowship shared with my neighbors and community.
Guide and sustain me that I may touch and love, laugh and
cry and give hope to myself and to others. Amen.*

Concentrate on listing only the positive things.

The positive things in my life.

1. _____

2. _____

3. _____

4. _____

5. _____

6. _____

7. _____

8. _____

9. _____

10. _____

Day 11

"Therefore the Lord waits to be gracious to you; therefore he exalts himself to show mercy to you." (Isaiah 30:18)

Today I will remember that life is filled with blessings as well as heartaches.

O Lord, I give thanks for your faithfulness to me, especially when I have been afraid to face the future. Sometimes there seems to be little on which I can place my hope. My mind knows that there will always be challenging times and some days will be harder to bear than others. Help me to look for the blessings even on those difficult days. Thank you for loving me and being patient with me as I seek to grow in my faith and love for others. Amen.

Count your many blessings. List them one by one.

My many blessings counted one by one.

1. _____

2. _____

3. _____

4. _____

5. _____

6. _____

7. _____

8. _____

9. _____

10. _____

Day 12

"As the Father has loved me, so have I loved you; abide in my love."   (John 15:9)

Today I will remember all those who love me and hold and support me in their prayers.

O Lord, I remember how you touched those who were sick, lonely and in need of a friend. Help me to be receptive to the patience and caring of family and friends as they share in my grief. May I yield to their love and to you, allowing you even now to mold me and make me into what I can become as I face an uncertain future. Amen.

Give thanks as you list the names of those who continue to provide support during these difficult times.

Individuals/groups who are now providing support.

1. _____

2. _____

3. _____

4. _____

5. _____

6. _____

7. _____

8. _____

9. _____

10. _____

Day 13

"May the God of hope fill you with all joy and peace in believing, so that by the power of the Holy Spirit you may abound in hope."   (Romans 15:13)

Today I promise myself that I will not give up.

O Lord, help me that I may continue to believe in the future. Sometimes I am inclined to give up when all I really need is to rest and turn things over to you. I want so much to believe that happiness will return sometime in my life. I do know that you will never give up on me; that you are ready and willing to guide me if I but ask. I believe; help my unbelief. Amen.

List the things from the past that you wish to hold on to as a part of today and the days and years yet to come.

Things from the past that I want to keep.

1. _____

2. _____

3. _____

4. _____

5. _____

6. _____

7. _____

8. _____

9. _____

10. _____

Day 14

"Behold, I make all things new."   (Revelation 21:5)

Today I place my life in your hands as I concentrate on new beginnings.

O Lord, remind me often that every day is new. Help me to remember that with each new dawn there will be delivered to my door a fresh, new package called "today." Help me to take hold of each "today" filled with its new opportunities, new hopes, new endeavors and new challenges. I know that the past cannot be changed but there can be a future for me if I will just place my life in your hands. Thank you for making me whole again. Amen

Sit quietly as you envision the future. When you are ready, record some of your hopes and dreams. Return to the listing from time to time and remember that even if they haven't all been realized God is still holding you in the palms of his hands.

My hopes and dreams for the future.

1. _____

2. _____

3. _____

4. _____

5. _____

6. _____

7. _____

8. _____

9. _____

10. _____

Special Memories

True friends will always remain
in each other's heart.

Visitors—Friends, Neighbors and Colleagues

Telephone Calls Received—Local and Long Distance

Flowers Received Before and After Funeral

Individuals and Groups Who Provided Food or Other Items

Individuals and Groups Who Met Special Needs

Other Books by Dorothy D. France

Toward Better Grouping for Reading—*Editorial Committee*

Special Days of the Church Year

Newness of Life

Go Quickly and Tell—*Contributor*

Partners in Prayer (Advent)

Welcome to the United States—An Orientation Guide
    for Refugees

At Christ's Table—Meditations and Prayers for
    Communion

Blessed Assurance—Fifty-two Meditations Inspired by
    Familiar Hymns of the Church

You Might Be A Football Fan If . . . with Jason and
    David Frankle

You Might Be A Basketball Fan If . . . with Jason and
    David Frankle